ANIMALS
HERE WE GROW!

Shelley Rotner

HOLIDAY HOUSE · NEW YORK

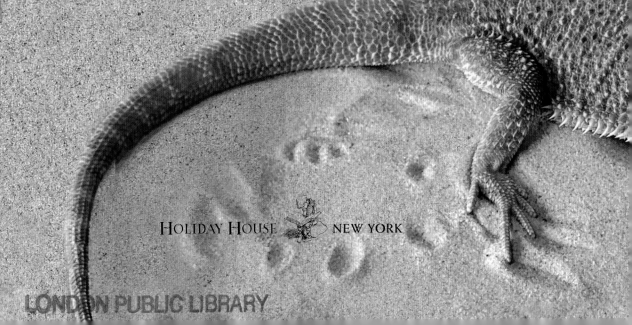

Animals
change
as
they
grow . . .

Egg to caterpillar to chrysalis to butterfly.

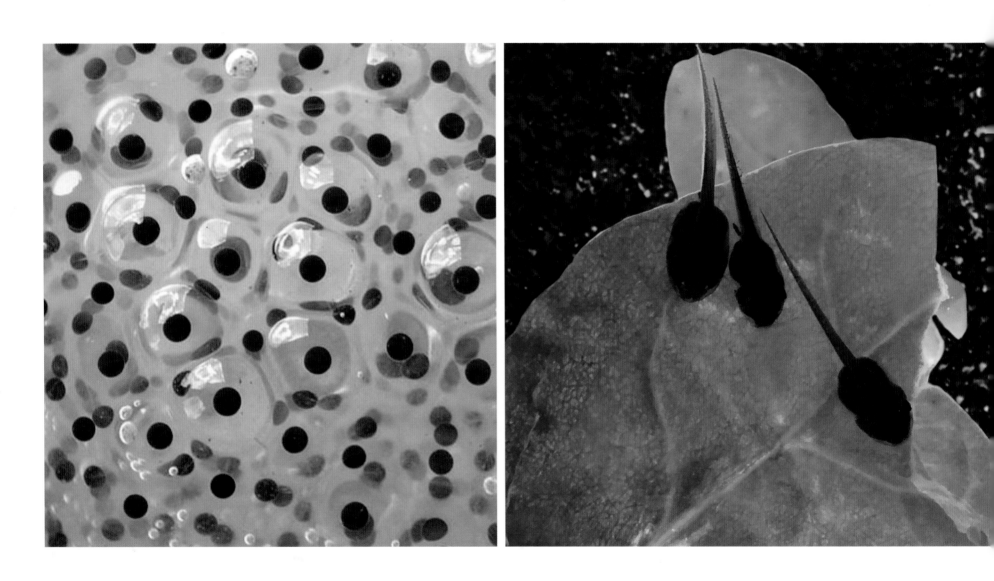

Egg to tadpole to frog.

Egg to hatchling to chick to bird.

Egg to hatchling to chick to chicken.

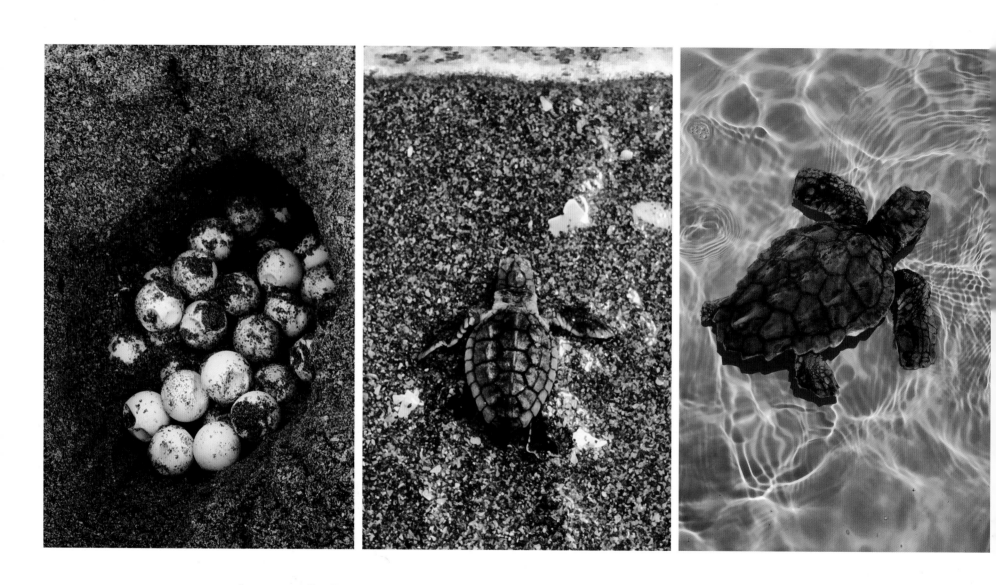

Egg to hatchling to turtle.

Egg to hatchling to snake.

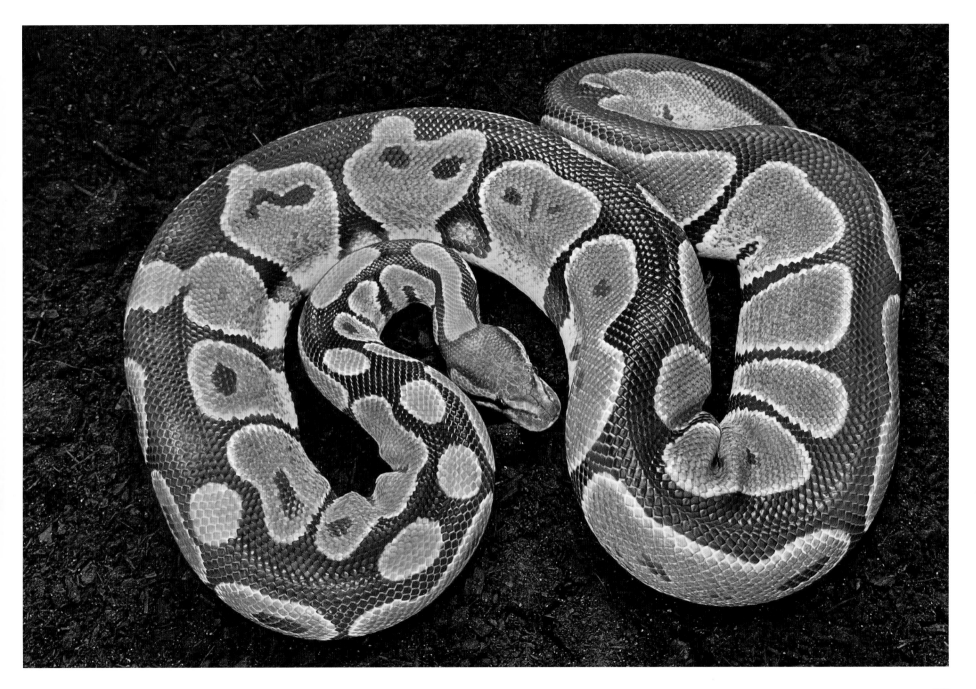

Egg to hatchling to lizard.

Kit to rabbit.

Piglet to pig.

Lamb to sheep.

Foal to colt to stallion.

Kitten to cat.

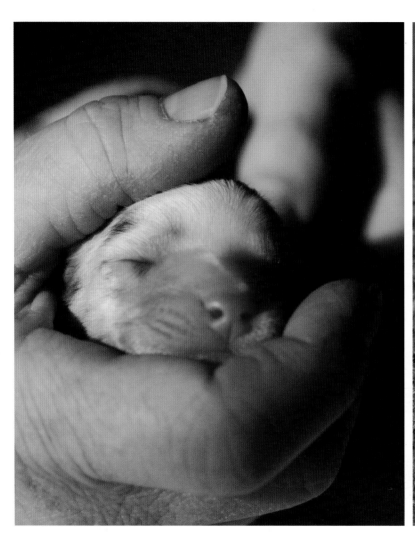

Puppy to dog.

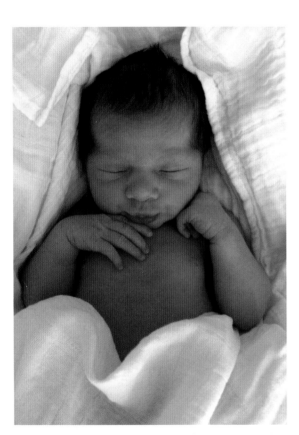

People change as they grow too.

LIFE CYCLES

All animals go through changes as they grow.

Different animals have different life cycles.

Some look like small adults when they are born and just keep on growing until they reach their full size. Others have distinct stages of growth and look different at each stage.

An animal may start as an egg, hatch into a caterpillar, then form a chrysalis, and finally emerge as an adult as a butterfly.

The series of changes or stages from birth to death is called a life cycle and repeats for each new generation.

Butterfly

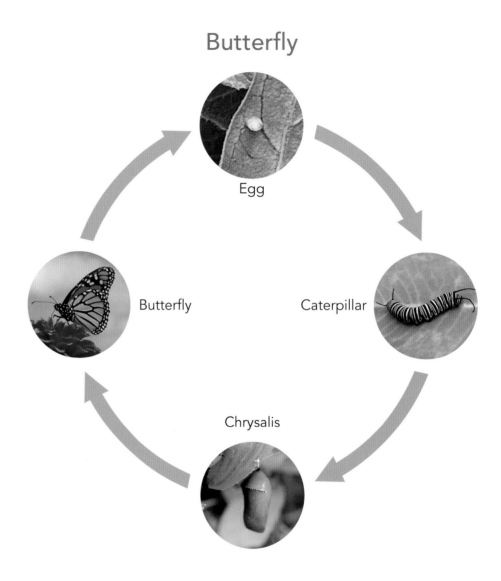

Egg

Caterpillar

Chrysalis

Butterfly

Bird

Frog

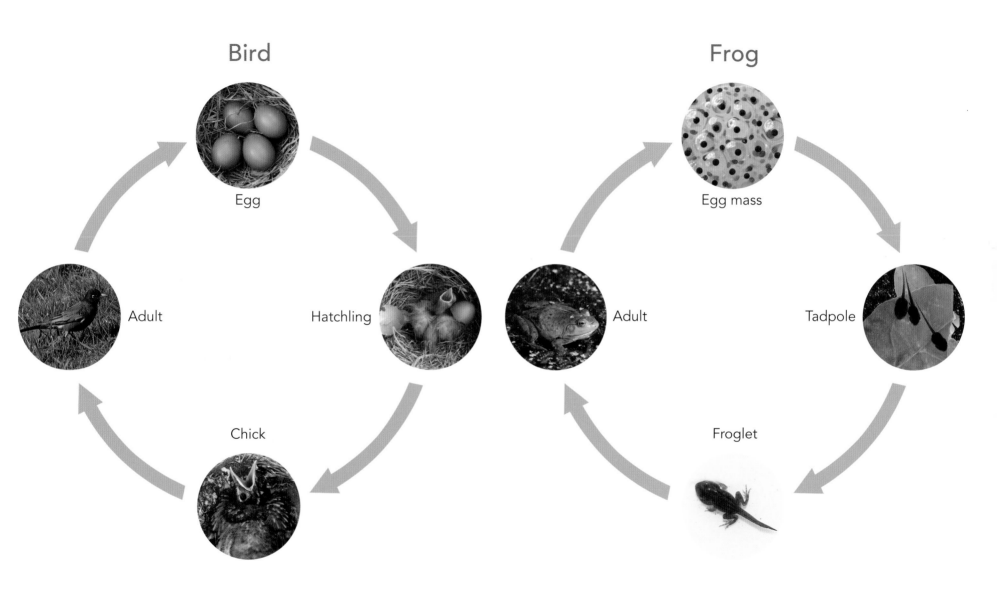

Egg

Hatchling

Adult

Chick

Egg mass

Tadpole

Adult

Froglet

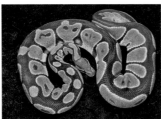

GLOSSARY

Breed
A group of animals that belong to the same species that look alike and are alike in other ways.

Chyrsalis
A stage of development in the life cycle of some insects. It is a hard covering that protects a caterpillar as it changes into a butterfly.

Generation
A complete cycle of life from birth to death of any animal.

Hatchling
A baby that comes out of an egg.

Life span
The length of time an animal lives.

Metamorphosis
The different stages of development that an animal goes through.

To Charlie and to the joy it brings me watching you grow!

Special thanks to Rob at Zoo Creatures.

Design: Michael Grinley

Fawn

Buck

Printed and bound in November 2020 at Leo Paper, Heshan, China. | www.holidayhouse.com | First Edition | 1 3 5 7 9 10 8 6 4 2
Library of Congress Cataloging-in-Publication Data
Names: Rotner, Shelley, author. | Title: Animals! here we grow / Shelley Rotner. | Description: First edition. | New York : Holiday House, [2021] | Audience:
Ages 3-7 | Audience: Grades K-1 | Summary: "Photographs document the life cycle of a variety of mammals, insects, birds, amphibians, and reptiles"—Provided by publisher.
Identifiers: LCCN 2020005942 | ISBN 9780823448289 (hardcover) | Subjects: LCSH: Animal life cycles—Juvenile literature. | Classification: LCC QL49 .R637 2021
DDC 571.8—dc23 | LC record available at https://lccn.loc.gov/2020005942 | ISBN: 978-0-8234-4828-9 (hardcover)